Ilvago
S. Vettor
Perarolo
Corlaneon
Laguiaro
Caldero
Villa noua
Zimella
Baldar
Vo
Progno
Villa bella
S. Stefano
Cologna
El finale
Gombion
S. Bonifacio
S. Felice
Nouenta
Villa broia
Porul
Sabion
Persana
S. Andrea
Jolana
Vall di cor
S. Maria
Adese flu.
Bionde
La Cucha
Roueredo
Ciole
Fiume nouo
toncelo
Arcole
Casela
Fraßene
Fresto
Zeuio
Zerpa
Pont Zerpan
Masaran
To Rabiosa
S. Sebastiano
Pra da boce
Spedalett
Periaco
Ladesmonta
Pra da boce
S. Margarita
Ca dal bosco
Roncha
Caneuera
S. Sebastiano
Saletto
Valure
Calca neg
Albano
Canton
Albare
Beuilacqua
S. Fenee
nga
Tomba
Riualta
S. Zenon
Montagnan
Vale
Palu
Corso
S. Thoma
Menerbe
Saluro
lon
Corian
Orbana
reda
L'Olmo
Becaciueta
S. Stefano
Marega
Merlara
Val de Pi azen
Vigazo
Opean
Bonauigo
Horti
Bosco
za
lo lage
Busse A.
Rouechiura
Isola porcariza
Terrazzo
alese
S. Pierro
Porto
Visara
Ter Fate. va
Angiari
Lenago
Bogore
To Bana
Piacenz
Balduina
ac Opij
Malauesina
Villa Bartholomei
Nichesola
Termini
C. Baldo
Vila f
S. Piero
Vigo
Carpi
atana
Paganina
Vang aea
Villa bona
Badia
Rafa
Menago fl.
Cerca
Ponzina
Castagnara
M. Peson
Saluatera
Aspare
Aselongna
Nichelola. A.
Baruchela
Canda
Concamarise
Ronco
Tartaro A.
Casalauon
Buolosi
se
Trezeua
Bagnol
Casa lauon
Aspreta
Crocetta
Carpe
Sanguene
Castagnaro
Ronei
La Borgesana
Fossa Gualandro
La Daniela
Valle del Verone flu.
Zelo
Freshnun A.
Ceua
Tartaro flu.
Bastion de la Crosetta
Villa noua
Seri
a
Bagna
Ospedaleto
Macacari
Tizardo
Canal
Stienta

ROMEO & JULIET

ROMEO &

RETOLD BY ANDREA HOPKINS

JULIET

ILLUSTRATIONS BY MARINE D'ANTIBES

BARNES
&NOBLE
BOOKS
NEW YORK

ONG AGO IN THE BEAUTIFUL CITY OF VERONA
lived two rich and noble families, the Montagues and the
Capulets. They had been mortal enemies for so long that
no one could remember the cause of their original quarrel; but that
didn't really matter anymore—hatred had become such a habit with
them, that if the young men of the Capulet clan happened to see
the young men of the Montague clan in the streets of Verona, they
would immediately draw their swords and start fighting. Even their
servants would scream insults at one another and sometimes provoke a brawl. The people of Verona were pretty tired of the feud;
they could hardly go about their business without having to run
from a swordfight. And the Prince of Verona, the noble Escalus,
was very tired of it—he wanted peace in the streets, and both families were constantly flouting his laws.

LORD MONTAGUE HAD ONLY ONE SON, Romeo. He was young, handsome, impulsive, and passionate. He wasn't much interested in the family feud, because something new had just come into his life—the painful pleasures of being in love. The lady he had decided to be in love with was called Rosaline. She was very beautiful, but cold and distant. She paid no attention to Romeo's sighs and declarations. Romeo dedicated himself to his misery. He took to getting up before sunrise and walking alone in deserted gardens, weeping; and when daylight came, he would lock himself in his room with the curtains drawn. Romeo's friend and cousin, Benvolio, asked him the reason for his odd behavior. Hearing that Romeo was in love with a lady who didn't care one bit for him, Benvolio advised him to get out more and see other beautiful ladies—and in particular, to come with him to a party that Lord Capulet was giving that same evening. It happened that Rosaline would be there, so Romeo agreed to go to the party (in disguise, of course) so that he could see her.

Lord Capulet was giving this party so that his only daughter Juliet could meet the young Count Paris. He was a very handsome and wealthy young nobleman; he had seen Juliet, fallen in love with her, and asked her father for permission to marry her. Lord Capulet was very happy with the idea of Count Paris as a son-in-law; he was everything a father could desire. But he was in no hurry to have Juliet married off. She was very young—not quite fourteen years old—and although people got married much younger in those days, that was still young. Lord Capulet kindly told the eager count that if he could get to know Juliet, woo her, and get her to like him, then he would allow the marriage to take place.

Romeo, Benvolio, and their friend Mercutio arrived at the house of Lord Capulet wearing masks, so that they would not be recognized. Mercutio was teasing Romeo about being in love, and Romeo was answering him back in a fine witty vein, when they were confronted by the sight of all the ladies and gentlemen at the feast dancing by torchlight. In the center of the beautiful scene danced Juliet, and the sight of her beauty struck Romeo to his very soul. He forgot that he was in the house of his mortal enemy; he couldn't help speaking aloud his admiration:

O, she doth teach the torches to burn bright!
It seems she hangs upon the cheek of night
As a rich jewel in an Ethiop's ear:
Beauty too rich for use, for earth too dear!...
Did my heart love till now? Forswear it, sight!
For I ne'er saw true beauty till this night.

Unfortunately he happened to be standing near a young man named Tybalt, Juliet's cousin and one of the fiercest and most aggressive of the younger Capulets. He recognized Romeo by his voice as a Montague, and was just getting ready to run him through with his sword, when old Lord Capulet stopped him.

In a benign mood, the old lord did not want brawling and bloodshed to spoil his feast; and Tybalt's determination to punish Romeo only provoked Lord Capulet's annoyance with Tybalt himself. While they stood arguing, Romeo took the opportunity to approach Juliet and speak to her:

If I profane with my unworthiest hand
This holy shrine, the gentle sin is this:
My lips, two blushing pilgrims, ready stand
To smooth that rough touch with a tender kiss.

FOR A FEW MOMENTS the two were caught up in a little world of their own, as each was bewitched by the presence of the other. Juliet was equally attracted to Romeo; it wasn't long before he had stolen a kiss from her, and he was just about to snatch another, when Juliet's nurse called her away to speak to her mother. Romeo, still not knowing who Juliet was, asked the nurse, and learned to his dismay that his new love was the daughter of his bitterest enemy. Romeo and his friends decided to depart, and as they were just going out of the gate, Juliet sent her nurse to discover Romeo's identity. When the nurse told Juliet that Romeo was a member of the hated Montague clan, she lamented:

> *My only love sprung from my only hate!*
> *Too early seen unknown, and known too late.*
> *Prodigious birth of love it is to me,*
> *That I must love a loathèd enemy.*

With that, Juliet was called away to bed.

Romeo was overwhelmed by the power of his feelings. He couldn't bear to leave the place where Juliet lived, and he also didn't want to be with his friends just then and have to listen to all their jokes—especially from the sharp-tongued Mercutio—so he hid until they had gone on without him.

Then he climbed over the wall into the orchard at the back of the Capulets' house, and almost at once caught sight of Juliet, who had come to her bedroom window to look out into the night. Once more the force of his love burst out in speech:

> But soft! What light through yonder window breaks?
> It is the east, and Juliet is the sun!
> Arise, fair sun, and kill the envious moon,
> Who is already sick and pale with grief
> That thou, her maid, art far more fair than she. . . .
> It is my lady. O! It is my love!
> O that she knew she were! . . .
> See how she leans her cheek upon her hand:
> O that I were a glove upon that hand,
> That I might touch that cheek.

Juliet, too, was overwhelmed by her feelings of love for her father's enemy, so briefly seen and so suddenly adored. She came out onto the balcony of her room to speak her thoughts aloud, and Romeo was overjoyed to hear her confess that she loved him. His being one of the Montagues was her only grief:

> *O Romeo, Romeo! wherefore art thou Romeo?*
> *Deny thy father, and refuse thy name;*
> *Or, if thou wilt not, be but sworn my love,*
> *And I'll no longer be a Capulet. . . .*
> *What's in a name? That which we call a rose*
> *By any other name would smell as sweet;*
> *So Romeo would, were he not Romeo called,*
> *Retain that dear perfection which he owes . . .*

On hearing this, Romeo could contain himself no longer, and stepped out from under the trees into the bright moonlight where Juliet could see him. He proclaimed that the strength of his new devotion was such that he would gladly renounce his family name if Juliet returned his love:

> *Call me but love, and I'll be new baptis'd;*
> *Henceforth I never will be Romeo.*

Juliet at first was frightened to find that she had been overheard, but she quickly recognized Romeo's voice, although she had heard so few words spoken by him before; and then she was frightened for a new reason—that her kinsmen might come along, find Romeo, and kill him. In answer to all her questions—how did he get into the orchard, how did he find her room, why had he come?—Romeo replied that love and only love had brought him to her, and that he would dare anything for her sake:

I am no pilot; yet, wert thou as far
As that vast shore wash'd with the farthest sea,
I would adventure for such merchandise.

It was useless for Juliet to deny her feelings and play hard to get, since Romeo had overheard her secret confession, so she gladly though a little fearfully admitted that she loved him too. She worried that he might think her too easily won, but promised him that she would be as true as if their courtship had been more difficult and long drawn out. Yet she was afraid to trust her feelings, and tried to escape indoors:

I have no joy of this contract tonight:
It is too rash, too unadvis'd, too sudden;
Too like the lightning, which doth cease to be
Ere one can say "It lightens!" Sweet, good-night!

But Romeo begged her not to leave him so soon, and they spoke again of their true love, passion, and their newfound joy. Then Juliet's nurse called her from inside the house, and she had to go, but she promised to come out again in a minute. When she reappeared, all her doubts had vanished; her love was too great for doubting either herself or Romeo. Where could such happiness and ardor lead, but to marriage? Juliet herself proposed it as the inevitable goal of their love:

If that thy bent of love be honourable,
Thy purpose marriage, send me word tomorrow,
By one that I'll procure to come to thee,
Where and what time thou wilt perform the rite;
And all my fortunes at thy foot I'll lay,
And follow thee my lord throughout the world.

*A*ND STILL THEY COULDN'T bear to say goodnight. Juliet came back out to the balcony after going in to her nurse, and called Romeo back from climbing the wall to speak yet again of their love. At last, when it was nearly morning, she went inside. Romeo bid her a last farewell:

Parting is such sweet sorrow
That I shall say goodnight till it be morrow.

Romeo was no longer inclined to brood and dwell on his feelings. He had something to do—organize a secret wedding. It was of course out of the question to ask Juliet's father for her hand in marriage in the proper way; they would have to elope. Fortunately, Romeo had a friend, a monk named Friar Laurence, who lived alone in a simple cell outside Verona. Romeo went directly to him after leaving Juliet—though it was so early in the morning, Friar Laurence was already up gathering flowers. He had always disapproved of Romeo's infatuation for Rosaline, and had tried many times to talk him out of it, but Romeo trusted him to see the difference between that imagined passion and the real love that he felt for Juliet, and asked for his help. Friar Laurence was reluctant to believe that the old love could so quickly be driven out by the new, but he was a good-hearted and well-meaning old man, and one thing he did understand was that this marriage might be a chance to put an end to the wicked and wasteful struggle between the two families, and bring them together in peace. So he agreed to marry Romeo and Juliet later that same day.

AFTER HIS MEETING WITH FRIAR LAURENCE, Romeo was in high spirits. He met with his close friends Mercutio and Benvolio, but he did not take them into his confidence about Juliet or his plans. Their talk was all joking and jesting and making fun. When Juliet's old nurse arrived, whom Juliet had sent out to find Romeo and learn of the wedding plans, Mercutio teased her mercilessly. But Romeo managed to tell her that Juliet must meet him at Friar Laurence's cell that very afternoon, and he arranged for his servant Balthasar to give the nurse a rope-ladder that she could let down from Juliet's balcony that night, so that Romeo could climb up and be with her.

Juliet had her parents' permission to visit Friar Laurence to make her confession; little did they know that she went out a maid and came back a married woman. The two lovers were dazed by their happiness, and Romeo passionately expressed his feelings for Juliet:

Ah Juliet, if the measure of thy joy
Be heap'd like mine, and that thy skill be more
To blazon it, then sweeten with thy breath
This neighbour air, and let rich music's tongue

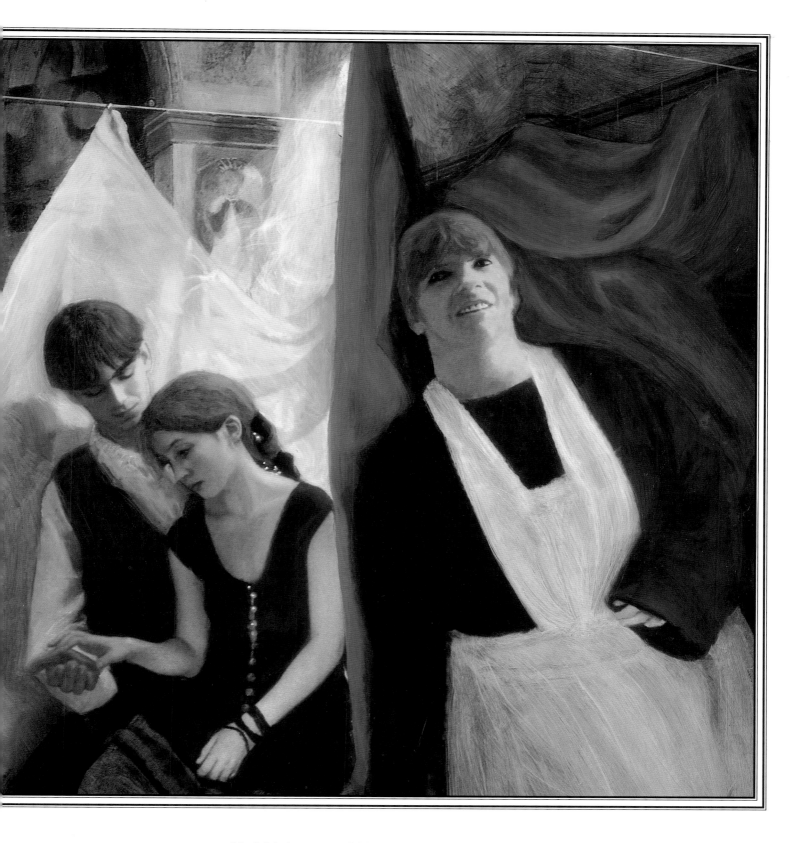

Unfold the imagin'd happiness that both
Receive in either by this dear encounter.

In response, Juliet declared that she treasured her love for Romeo more than anything else in the world.

FRIAR LAURENCE quickly married them. They eagerly looked forward to the joys that would come with nightfall; but before that Juliet had to return to her father's house, and Romeo went back into the city to meet his friends. And then a terrible thing occurred.

Tybalt, the angry young man of Juliet's family, had burned with resentment against Romeo ever since he had discovered him in disguise at the Capulets' feast. He met with Mercutio and Benvolio in the streets of Verona, and they were bandying words, when Romeo arrived. Tybalt immediately called Romeo a villain, to provoke him to fight; but Romeo, conscious that now Tybalt was his kinsman by marriage, was very unwilling to fight, maybe to hurt or even kill, one of Juliet's close family. So he answered all Tybalt's insults calmly and reasonably, hoping to avert an open battle. This enraged his good friend Mercutio, who himself took up Tybalt's challenge to a duel, and the two sprang at one another with drawn swords. In vain Romeo reminded them that the Prince had forbidden fighting in the streets, and in the end he had to physically get between them and knock their swords in the air before they would stop. But Tybalt, the hot-blooded, angry Tybalt, could not resist one last thrust, and buried his sword deep in Mercutio's side. Mercutio fell into Romeo's arms. His wound did not look like much, but he felt that it was fatal. Even as he lay dying, he couldn't resist a joke:

. . . 'tis not so deep as a well, nor so wide as a church door; but 'tis enough, 'twill serve. Ask for me tomorrow, and you shall find me a grave man. . . . Why the devil came you between us? I was hurt under your arm. . . .

A plague o' both your houses. They have made worms' meat of me. . . .

ENVOLIO HELPED MERCUTIO into a nearby house, leaving Romeo bitterly regretting his restraint toward Tybalt. Soon Benvolio came back with the dreadful news that Mercutio had died of his wound. Romeo was devastated. He felt responsible for his friend's death, and very angry with Tybalt. At that moment Tybalt chose to reappear, and Romeo turned on him furiously:

> *Now Tybalt, take the "villain" back again*
> *That late thou gav'st me; for Mercutio's soul*
> *Is but a little way above our heads,*
> *Staying for thine to keep him company:*
> *Either thou, or I, or both, must go with him.*

Tybalt was happy to oblige, and the two young men fell on each other furiously. Romeo in his anger was too much for Tybalt, and before a minute of rapid swordplay had passed, he fell dead to the ground. By this time the citizens had sent for the Prince and his soldiers to stop the fight, and Benvolio hurried his friend away before the Prince could throw him into jail, or worse. Soon the Prince arrived, hot on the heels of the Montagues and the Capulets, each blaming the other and crying for blood—the Capulets demanding Romeo's death in payment for Tybalt's, and the Montagues shouting that Tybalt had gotten his just desserts for murdering Mercutio. The Prince, goaded beyond endurance by this latest outrage, banished Romeo from Verona. If he should ever be found inside the city walls again, he would die.

Meanwhile, Juliet was feeling an intense, physical longing for her new husband:

> *Come, gentle night; come, loving, black-brow'd night,*
> *Give me my Romeo. And when I shall die*
> *Take him and cut him out in little stars,*

And he will make the face of heaven so fine
That all the world will be in love with night
And pay no worship to the garish sun.

But then came Juliet's nurse, with the awful news that Tybalt had been killed by Romeo, who was now banished from Verona on pain of death. At first, on hearing the news that Romeo had killed her cousin, Juliet was very upset and expressed bitter anger towards Romeo:

O serpent heart, hid with a flowering face!
Did ever dragon keep so fair a cave?
Beautiful tyrant! fiend angelical!…
A damnèd saint, an honourable villain!…
Was ever book containing such vile matter
So fairly bound? O that deceit should dwell
In such a gorgeous palace.

ER NURSE, SYMPATHIZING with her spontaneous grief, began to abuse Romeo as well, and Juliet leaped like a tigress to his defense. This made her realize that she loved Romeo in spite of his slaying of Tybalt, and turned her grief to grim pleasure that Tybalt, who would have killed Romeo if he could, had perished in the attempt. But at last she remembered that Nurse had also said that because of the fight, Romeo had been banished—and this was the real cause for grief. Her tears burst out anew, and she passionately vowed that she would not live long without him. At this Nurse offered to go and find Romeo, and at whatever risk, bring him back with her into the city. Juliet eagerly encouraged her:

> O, find him! Give this ring to my true knight,
> And bid him come to take his last farewell.

Romeo was at Friar Laurence's cell, where the good friar told him the news of the Prince's judgment, that he was banished from Verona. Friar Laurence told him he should think himself lucky only to be banished, since by the strict letter of the law he should have been executed for killing Tybalt. But Romeo didn't see things that way. For him, permanent separation from Juliet was worse than death—life without her was not worth living. Juliet's nurse arrived to find Romeo face down on the ground, weeping and grinding his teeth with grief and rage at the unlucky way things had turned out. He asked how his beloved Juliet was:

> . . . How is it with her?
> Doth not she think me an old murderer,
> Now I have stain'd the childhood of our joy
> With blood remov'd but little from her own?
> Where is she? and how doth she? and what says
> My conceal'd lady to our cancell'd love?

Nurse told him that Juliet was devastated, weeping for both him and Tybalt. When he heard this, Romeo was close to despair at the very thought of having given Juliet such pain, and almost drew his sword to kill himself. But the friar spoke firmly to Romeo, advising him not to give way to his feelings, but to have courage and look on the bright side; after all, the chief threat to his life and liberty had been Tybalt, and Tybalt was now out of the way forever. Juliet, his love, was still alive, and needed him to go to

her and comfort her. He should spend the night with her, but leave to go to some friends in Mantua before the patrol of the morning watch. So Romeo crept secretly back into Verona to spend his wedding night with his beloved Juliet. And that night was far too short for either of them; between their joy in each other's love and their grief about their imminent parting, the minutes and the hours raced by before they knew it. Then it was daybreak, and Romeo had to set off—it was too dangerous for him to stay any longer.

BY A CRUEL TRICK OF FATE, Count Paris had been to see old Lord Capulet and had gotten him to promise that he could marry Juliet in three days' time. Perhaps the slaying of Tybalt had changed the old lord's mind about her being too young, and made him think it desirable to place her under the protection of someone young and able-bodied. No sooner had Romeo climbed back over the orchard wall that morning and disappeared from her sight than Juliet's mother came into her daughter's bedroom to tell her what her father had planned for her. Juliet showed great presence of mind in pretending to her mother that she hated Romeo for killing her cousin Tybalt; but she was so shocked by the idea of marrying Paris that she simply refused to do it. Her father came in and was so enraged that his careful plans for her should be so bluntly rejected, that he threatened to throw her out on the street if she would not obey him.

*I*N HER PANIC, JULIET RAN TO FRIAR LAURENCE and begged him to advise and help her. He had an idea, but he warned her that it was a desperate and fearful remedy—did she have the courage to carry it through? Juliet assured him that she would rather hide in a burial vault with rattling skeletons than break faith with her Romeo by marrying someone else. Then the friar gave her a little bottle of liquid, and advised her to go home and pretend to go along with her father's wishes and be glad to marry Count Paris; but the night before the wedding, she must lie alone in her room, without even her faithful nurse, and drink the liquid in the bottle. It would deprive her of warmth and breath, and put her into a coma so deep that everyone would think her dead. Then she would be buried, as was the custom, in the Capulet family vault. But the effects would last for only forty-two hours, and by that time, Friar Laurence promised, he would send a messenger to Mantua to summon Romeo and together they would wait beside her until she woke up, and she could then return to Mantua with Romeo. Juliet eagerly agreed.

On the way back from seeing Friar Laurence she met her father, and meekly told him of her change of heart. In his joy, he moved the wedding up a day, and that very evening Juliet found herself alone in her room and faced with the little bottle. What if the potion didn't work? Juliet promised that she would stab herself in the heart rather than marry Count Paris. What if it were really poison? But the friar was a good and honest man; he would never lie to her. What if she should awaken early, and find herself in the tomb alone, no Romeo waiting for her,

> *Where for these many hundred years the bones*
> *Of all my buried ancestors are pack'd;*
> *Where bloody Tybalt, yet but green in earth,*
> *Lies festering in his shroud; where, as they say,*
> *At some hours in the night, spirits resort!*

Would she not go mad with terror? But Juliet recognized that the terrors caused by her own imagination were more real than any other threat, and to escape these she drank the potion, and fell lifeless on her bed.

In the early morning her old nurse came to wake her, and found her cold and stiff in seeming death. Her shrieks and cries brought Juliet's mother, and then her father, who cried:

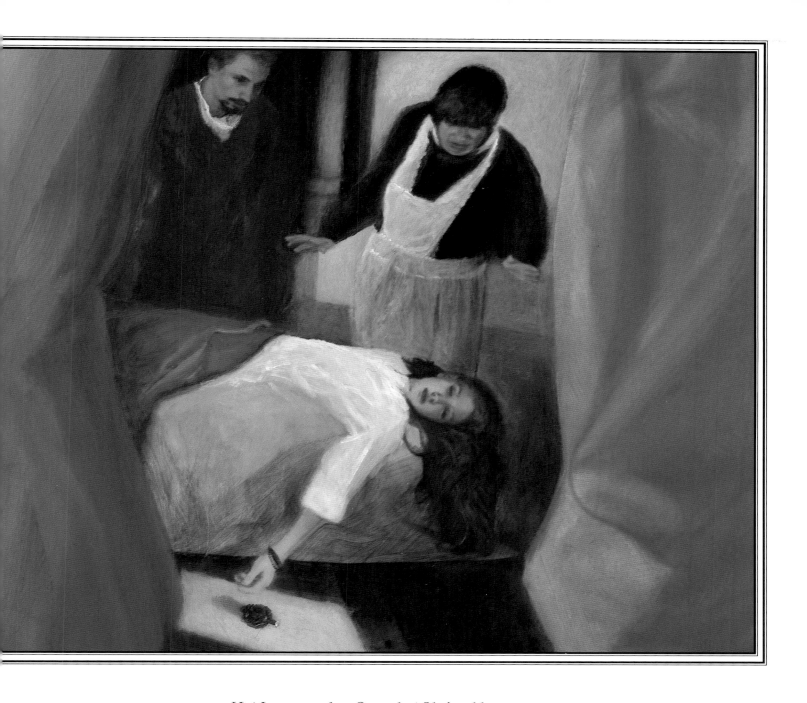

Ha! Let me see her. Out, alas! She's cold;
Her blood is settled, and her joints are stiff;
Life and these lips have long been separated:
Death lies on her like an untimely frost
Upon the sweetest flower of all the field. . . .
O child! O child! My soul, and not my child!
Dead art thou! Alas, my child is dead,
And with my child my joys are buried!

IN SPITE OF THEIR ANGER with her when she was disobedient, Juliet's father and mother loved her deeply and were heartbroken by her apparent death. She was their only child. And so the hastily prepared wedding celebrations were changed into a funeral; the garlands of flowers became funeral wreaths, the wedding breakfast became a sad funeral gathering, and the musicians hired to make merry were instructed to play mournful music. Then Friar Laurence arrived to conduct the ceremony, and Juliet was borne to church, never to leave again.

Romeo's manservant Balthasar saw all this. Not knowing the truth, he rode off immediately to Mantua to tell the dreadful news to his master. Friar Laurence's messenger, meanwhile, had been prevented from finding Romeo and delivering the all-important letter that would have explained that Juliet was not really dead, but was asleep.

NO WORDS CAN EXPRESS Romeo's agony on hearing that his adored young wife was dead. Yet his reaction was strangely calm, because it was clear to him that there was only one thing to do—return to Verona, break into the vault, and die by Juliet's side. His only question was, how was he to kill himself? After a little thought, he remembered a poor apothecary who lived nearby, whose shop was full of dusty old stuffed reptiles and bones, but all the shelves were bare of goods. It was forbidden, on pain of death, to sell poison in Mantua, but Romeo knew that this man was so poor, starving, miserable, and desperate, that he would break the law for money. Romeo bought the lethal poison and set off at once.

At the tomb, Romeo gave Balthasar a letter addressed to his father and sent him away to deliver it; but Balthasar, fearing some awful event would occur, stayed to watch. The tomb was not deserted. Count Paris, too, had loved Juliet, and he had come alone but for one page boy, to say his last farewell and strew flowers about her grave. Hearing Romeo's footsteps, he hid, but when he saw Romeo breaking open the entrance to the tomb, he recognized him, stepped forward, and tried to arrest him. Romeo was almost past patience at this last obstacle to his goal of togetherness with Juliet.

He tried to answer patiently, warning Paris:

> *Good gentle youth, tempt not a desperate man;*
> *Fly hence and leave me. Think upon these gone;*
> *Let them affright thee. I beseech thee, youth,*
> *Put not another sin upon my head*
> *By urging me to fury. O, be gone:*
> *By heaven, I love thee better than myself.*

But Paris was determined, and in the end provoked Romeo to attack him. The little page boy, seeing them begin to fight, ran away to call the night watch. The two young men struggled briefly together, but Paris was no match for Romeo in his fury. Falling mortally wounded to the ground, the dying Paris begged Romeo to be merciful and let him lie in the tomb with Juliet.

Romeo sympathized with his dead rival and gently laid his body in the tomb. But the sight of Juliet drove everything else from his mind. He had not been prepared to find her beauty so little spoiled by death, and like the first time he saw her, it took his breath away:

> *... O my love, my wife!*
> *Death, that hath suck'd the honey of thy breath,*
> *Hath had no power yet upon thy beauty.*
> *Thou art not conquer'd; beauty's ensign yet*
> *Is crimson in thy lips and in thy cheeks,*
> *And death's pale flag is not advanced there.*

If only he had realized that Juliet's lifelike appearance in fact meant that she was not really dead! But he knew nothing of the friar's potion. He knelt beside his beloved Juliet, gazed on her still face, gathered her in his arms for one last embrace, and kissed her cold lips. Then, when his broken heart could stand no more, and he longed only to join her in death, he drank his poison and died beside her.

Friar Laurence, having learned that his message never reached Romeo, had hurried to the tomb so as to be present when the effects of the drug wore off and Juliet awoke. He now arrived and saw the light burning, the two bloody swords, and going in, found the bodies of Paris and Romeo. He had no time to do more than notice them, when Juliet began to awake from her drugged sleep.

What an awakening! There beside her was the dead body of her darling husband. Friar Laurence could hear that the night watchmen were coming, at last aroused by the lights and noise, and he dared not stay; he begged Juliet to come with him. But she had grown up very suddenly with the events of the last few days, and in a tone of voice not to be disobeyed, ordered him to leave her, for she would not abandon the body of her beloved. She knelt by him and said:

What's here? A cup, clos'd in my true love's hand?
Poison, I see, hath been his timeless end.
O churl! Drunk all, and left no friendly drop
To help me after! I will kiss thy lips;
Haply, some poison yet doth hang on them,
To make me die with a restorative.

At that, she heard the watch approaching and decided she could wait no longer. Seizing Romeo's dagger, she cried:

Yea noise? Then I'll be brief. O happy dagger.
This is thy sheath—there rust and let me die.

She fell back upon the body of Romeo and her life drained away. The watchmen arrived, with Count Paris's page, and found the ground trampled

and bloody. They soon found Romeo's man Balthasar, and Friar Laurence, and they immediately sent for Prince Escalus, who was quickly followed by a crowd of others, including the Capulets and Lord Montague.

Friar Laurence explained what had happened, and one by one they all told what they knew, and the sad story was made known. The Prince read Romeo's letter and then said:

> *Where be these enemies?—Capulet! Montague!*
> *See what a scourge is laid upon your hate,*
> *That heaven finds means to kill your joys with love;*
> *And I, for winking at your discords too,*
> *Have lost a brace of kinsmen. All are punished.*

*T*HEN THE TWO OLD lords in their sorrow at last forgave one another and clasped hands in friendship. Lady Montague had not lived to see the tragic death of her only son; her grief at his banishment had stopped her heart the night before. United in loss, the lords bent their heads in grief over the bodies of their children.

Each promised to put up a richly wrought statue of the other's child, as a lasting monument to their faithful love, destroyed by their fathers' hatred. The Prince spoke the last words:

A glooming peace this morning
with it brings;
The sun for sorrow will not show
his head.
Go hence, to have more talk of
these sad things:
Some shall be pardon'd, and
some punished:
For never was a story of more woe
Than this of Juliet and her Romeo.

ABOUT WILLIAM SHAKESPEARE

We know the basic details of Shakespeare's life: his birth in Stratford-upon-Avon in 1564; the documented marriages, births, and deaths of his family there; his years in London as an actor, playwright, and producer; and his death on his 52nd birthday in 1616. Yet of the man himself—a writer whose rich legacy includes 37 plays and 154 sonnets that have added more words to the English language than any other body of literary work—we know little of a personal nature. What makes Shakespeare great? Why are his plays still so popular and performed so often, on stage, film, and television, some 400 years after they were first written? Why does each succeeding generation find something new and exciting in those works, producing fresh stage versions of *Hamlet*, *Henry V,* or *Romeo and Juliet*? Perhaps it is because Shakespeare puts his characters in situations of timeless interest—unrequited love, thirst for revenge, forced marriage—and makes us feel their joys and their sufferings so fully that we think of them as real people, accessible to our understanding. The Bard of Avon may always remain a mystery, but the popularity of his works, which can be said to have influenced everyone writing in English since, will surely endure.

ABOUT THE AUTHOR

Andrea Hopkins won an open scholarship to study at Oxford University, and gained a double First in English. A keen enthusiast for medieval art, literature, and history, the topic of her doctoral dissertation was medieval romance. She has written a popular illustrated history book on medieval chivalry, *Knights* (Abbeville Press, 1990), and has acted as consulting editor for *Medieval Towns* in the *I Was There* children's series (Random House, 1992). She has also written *The Chronicles of King Arthur* (Viking Penguin, 1993), *The Book of Courtly Love* (HarperCollins, 1994), and a children's book, *Harald the Ruthless—Last of the Vikings* (Henry Holt, 1996). Her most recently published work is *Most Wise and Valiant Ladies* (Welcome Rain, 1997). She is presently completing a prose retelling of *Hamlet* for young readers, which will be published as a companion to this edition of *Romeo and Juliet,* and is writing a historical novel about Eleanor of Aquitaine. She works at Oxford University Press.

ABOUT THE ILLUSTRATOR

Marine D'Antibes is a native of Belgium. She graduated from the Institut Saint-Luc du Bruxelles, and went on to teach there. She currently holds a professorship at the Ecole de Recherche Graphique in Brussels. Her extensive knowledge of the traditions of Western art, combined with a contemporary sense of composition, helps define her powerful narrative style. In *Romeo and Juliet* she creates a highly dramatic effect, both realistic and vital, through a masterful harmonizing of concept and technique. She has also illustrated Prosper Mérimée's *Federigo,* and is completing the illustrations for a children's edition of *Les Misérables* to be published by Barnes & Noble Books. Her work has been selected for exhibition at the Children's Book Fair in Bologna. *Romeo and Juliet* is her first book published in English.

Originally published as *Romeo and Juliet* by Grimm Press, 1995
English language edition copyright © 1998 by Barnes & Noble, Inc.

This edition published by Barnes & Noble, Inc., by arrangement with Grimm Press Ltd., Taiwan

1998 Barnes & Noble Books

Illustrations copyright © 1995 by Marine D'Antibes
Cover and text design for English-language edition by Leah Lococo

ISBN 0-7607-0807-X

Printed and bound in Spain
97 98 99 00 01 M 9 8 7 6 5 4 3 2 1
GRAF

In Caffi
Bardolin
Cauagion
Campara
Cifan
Paftrengo
Laxire
Polo
Guſſolengo
S. Vi
da
Aquæ ſulfureæ
ebullientes
Saline
Cola
Palazzolo
Pacengo
Sandra
C. di Cauri
Peſchera
C. Nouo
Sona
Betola
lla
Caualcaze
lo
Lago
Fornelo
Ponte
zolengo
Suma cam:
pagna
Boſſobon
L'alpo
S. Lience
La cuſtoza
Menee flu.
Villa franca
Gerla
Bouegia
Valezo
Cauriana
Ifolalta
Sareno
Li quaderini
Monzacone
S. Zen
Malauezina
Le Mozacane
gamba:
orgetto
Tormeno
Louerbella
oito
Caftion
Marmirolo
Menео A.
S. Maria
olara
Curtaton
Mantua
Borgo S. Zorgi
 Ronco ferar
La ca del pozzo
Barpazo
er Gerardum
S. Martin

S. Ambroſio
Gargagnago
Ouaro
Ponton
hoſpedale:
to
S. Pierro
Pefcantina
Arce
Settimo
Fiozan
S. Sofia
C. Rotto
Roſele
Arbiezo
Nouare
Parona
La crofara
Marzana
Quinto
Aueſ
Quinzan
S. Felice
Pogian
Mefente
Nouagie
C. montorio

Chieuo zeci
Verona
Buri
S. Michel
Marcel
Ferace
Fibio A.
Tomba
Atheſis A.
Torre del boſſolo

S. Jacomo
Letobon
S. N
Ca di daui
S. Zuane
louatoto
Scudo Orlando
Ca della fiera
Caporala
Slmagnan
Boua
Sl Pozo
Be
Fragazola
Cirengei
Bagnol
Cirengei
Zera
Settimo
Zan
Buapreda
Tor a
Colmo
Piombazzo
Cafele
Rampin
Vigna
Mazzagana
Villa
Jl Grezan
Tor
Jsola della
Scala
Tarmaſia
Premala
Boue
C Nogarole
Treuenzolo
Salifola
Albaro
Gamadon
Predele
Fagnan
Erbo
S. Gabriel
Le hionde de
nfegne
Villetta
Bagnol
Poſſero
P.
La peregrina
Lingaza
Roncoleua
Curia lta
Sorga
Ulma
Bonfenar
Barabo
Li dui caftei
Moradega
Bignarel
Caftellaro
Pampur
Fattola
Nogaz
Villa groſſa
Predele
Canpala
S Pierro in
valle
Grazo
Ronca noua
la frigza